1.

\- \- 1

Summary...3

Chapter 2..6

Chapter 1: Introduction to YouTube for Teenage Boys
....9

Chapter 2: Crafting Your Identity and Content..........17

Chapter 3: Technical Foundations of a Successful Channel..24

Chapter 4: Engaging with Your Audience 32

Chapter 5: Leveraging Social Media Platforms 40

Chapter 6: Dealing with Criticism and Online Pressures..48

Chapter 7: Monetization Strategies 56

Chapter 8: Advanced Content Creation Techniques ..64

Chapter 9: Growing Beyond YouTube.......................72

Chapter 10: Interviews with Successful YouTubers ..81

Chapter 11: Practical Exercises for Aspiring YouTubers 90

Chapter 12: Conclusion - Embarking on Your YouTube Journey 97

Synopsis 105

    2.

    3.

    4.

    5.

    6.

    7.

    8.

    9.

    10.

    11.

    12.

    13.

    14.

    15.

    16.

Summary

Chapter 1: Introduction to YouTube for Teenage Boys

3

1.1 The Digital Landscape for Young Creators

3

1.2 Opportunities and Challenges on YouTube

5

1.3 Setting Realistic Goals and Expectations

7

Chapter 2: Crafting Your Identity and Content

9

2.1 Discovering Your Passion and Niche

9

2.2 Authenticity, Creativity, and Consistency

11

2.3 Understanding Your Audience

13

Chapter 3: Technical Foundations of a Successful Channel

15

3.1 Basics of Video Production and Editing

15

3.2 SEO Strategies for Maximum Visibility

17

3.3 Utilizing Analytics to Guide Content Strategy

19

Chapter 4: Engaging with Your Audience

21

4.1 Building a Community Around Your Channel

21

4.2 Effective Communication and Feedback Loops

23

4.3 Collaborations and Cross-Promotions

25

Chapter 5: Leveraging Social Media Platforms

27

5.1 Integrating Social Media into Your Growth Strategy

27

5.2 Best Practices for Each Platform

29

5.3 Managing Multiple Platforms Efficiently

31

Chapter 6: Dealing with Criticism and Online Pressures

33

6.1 Handling Negative Comments Constructively

33

6.2 Balancing School, Life, and YouTube

35

6.3 Maintaining Mental Health in the Digital Space

37

Chapter 7: Monetization Strategies
39

7.1 Understanding YouTube's Monetization Policies
39

7.2 Diversifying Income Streams as a Creator
41

7.3 Brand Partnerships and Sponsorships
43

Chapter 8: Advanced Content Creation Techniques
45

8.1 Storytelling and Visual Narratives
45

8.2 Advanced Editing Techniques for Engagement
47

8.3 Innovating with Trends While Staying True to Your Niche
49

Chapter 9: Growing Beyond YouTube
51

9.1 Expanding Your Brand to Other Mediums
51

9.2 Engaging with Fans Off-YouTube
53

9.3 Long-term Brand Building Strategies

55

Chapter 10: Interviews with Successful YouTubers

57

10.1 Lessons from Their Journeys

57

10.2 Diverse Paths to Success

59

10.3 Advice for Upcoming Creators

61

Chapter 11: Practical Exercises for Aspiring YouTubers

63

11.1 Identifying Your Unique Selling Proposition (USP)

63

11.2 Creating an Engaging First Video

65

11.3 Developing a Content Calendar

66

Chapter 12: Conclusion - Embarking on Your YouTube Journey

68

12.1 Recapitulating Key Learnings

12.2 Staying Motivated Through Ups and Downs
68

12.3 Looking Towards the Future
70

71

1
Introduction to YouTube for Teenage Boys

1.1 The Digital Landscape for Young Creators

The digital age has ushered in unprecedented opportunities for young creators, particularly teenage boys looking to carve out their own space on platforms like YouTube. This landscape is rich with possibilities but navigating it requires a nuanced understanding of both the technical and creative aspects of content creation. For teenage boys aspiring to become influential YouTubers, grasping the dynamics of this digital terrain is the first step towards turning their visions into reality.

At its core, the digital landscape for young creators is defined by its accessibility and immediacy. With just a smartphone or computer, teenagers can produce content that has the potential to reach millions worldwide. However, this ease of access also means a highly saturated market, where standing out demands not only creativity and talent but strategic thinking and persistence.

Understanding audience engagement is crucial in this environment. Teenage boys must learn to analyze trends and preferences within their target demographic while staying true to their authentic selves. This balance between authenticity and marketability is often what distinguishes successful channels.

Moreover, mastering the technical side of YouTube is equally important. SEO (Search Engine Optimization), thumbnail design, video editing skills, and an understanding of YouTube's algorithm can significantly enhance a channel's visibility and growth. These skills are not innate but can be developed through study and practice, highlighting the importance of continuous learning in a creator's journey.

- Navigating copyright issues and understanding monetization policies

- Engaging with viewers through comments and social media platforms
- Collaborating with other creators to expand audience reach

In addition to these practical aspects, young creators face unique psychological challenges. The pressure to consistently produce popular content can be overwhelming, making mental health awareness an essential part of a creator's toolkit. Learning how to deal with criticism constructively and maintain a healthy work-life balance are critical skills for long-term success.

The digital landscape for young creators on YouTube offers vast opportunities tempered by challenges that require both creative passion and practical strategies to overcome. For teenage boys embarking on this journey, understanding these dynamics is key to building a successful channel that not only grows in numbers but also enriches their personal development.

1.2 Opportunities and Challenges on YouTube

The journey of a teenage boy venturing into the world of YouTube is fraught with both immense opportunities and significant challenges. This digital platform offers a canvas for creativity, self-expression, and potentially lucrative career paths. However, navigating this landscape requires an understanding of its complexities and hurdles.

One of the most compelling opportunities YouTube presents is the ability to reach a global audience without the need for traditional gatekeepers like broadcasters or publishers. Teenage boys can share their passions, whether it's gaming, music, tutorials, or vlogs about their daily lives, with viewers from all corners of the globe. This democratization of content creation has enabled many young creators to build communities around shared interests, fostering a sense of belonging and engagement.

Moreover, YouTube has become a viable career path for many, offering various revenue streams such as ad revenue, sponsorships, merchandise sales, and memberships. For enterprising teenage boys, learning how to monetize their content effectively can not only provide financial rewards but also teach valuable skills in entrepreneurship and marketing.

- Mastering video production techniques to enhance content quality
- Navigating the complexities of building and maintaining an engaged audience
- Understanding YouTube's ever-evolving algorithm to maximize content visibility

However, these opportunities come with their own set of challenges. The vastness of YouTube means that competition is fierce. Standing out requires not only consistent high-quality content but also a unique voice or niche that resonates with viewers. Additionally, the pressure to maintain regular uploads can be daunting for young creators who must balance their online endeavors with academic responsibilities and personal development.

The issue of online negativity and cyberbullying also poses a significant challenge. Teenage boys must learn to navigate criticism constructively while safeguarding their mental health against harmful comments or feedback.

In conclusion, while YouTube offers teenage boys a platform for expression and potential career opportunities, success demands resilience, adaptability, and a strategic approach to content creation. Understanding these dynamics is crucial for any young creator aspiring to make an impact on this vibrant digital stage.

1.3 Setting Realistic Goals and Expectations

Embarking on a YouTube journey, especially for teenage boys, is an exciting venture that promises creative freedom and the potential for recognition or even financial gain. However, it's crucial to approach this path with realistic goals and expectations to ensure a healthy, productive experience. Understanding the landscape of YouTube is the first step in setting these realistic objectives.

Firstly, recognizing the time and effort required to create content that stands out is essential. Many successful YouTubers spend years developing their channel before seeing significant growth. Patience and persistence are key virtues in this regard. Teenage boys should set milestones that reflect a gradual progression rather than expecting overnight success.

- Acknowledge the learning curve involved in mastering video production and editing skills.
- Understand that building an engaged audience takes consistent effort over time.
- Accept that algorithm changes can affect visibility and adapt strategies accordingly.

Moreover, it's important to define success on YouTube in personal terms. While some may equate success with subscriber counts or views, others might find fulfillment in improving their communication skills or making meaningful connections with a niche community. Setting goals related to personal development can be more rewarding and sustainable in the long run.

Financial expectations also need careful consideration. While there are stories of YouTubers earning substantial incomes, these are often exceptions rather than the rule. A more pragmatic approach is to view any potential earnings as a bonus while focusing on content creation for passion or educational purposes.

In conclusion, entering the world of YouTube with realistic goals and expectations allows teenage boys to navigate its challenges more effectively while enjoying the process of content creation. By understanding what's achievable and maintaining a focus on personal growth and learning, young creators can build a rewarding experience on the platform, regardless of external metrics of success.

2

Crafting Your Identity and Content

2.1 Discovering Your Passion and Niche

At the heart of every successful YouTube channel lies a clear understanding of one's passion and niche. This foundational step is crucial for teenage boys embarking on their journey to become influential content creators. Identifying what you are genuinely passionate about not only fuels your creativity but also ensures that the process remains enjoyable and sustainable over time. Moreover, carving out a unique niche within the vast YouTube ecosystem allows creators to stand out and attract a dedicated audience.

Finding one's passion often involves introspection and experimentation. It requires asking oneself questions about hobbies, interests, or topics that evoke excitement or curiosity. For some, this could be gaming, technology, sports, education, or even daily vlogging about life as a teenager. The key is to identify subjects that you can talk about endlessly and with enthusiasm.

Once a broad area of interest is identified, narrowing down to a specific niche becomes imperative. This involves researching existing content on YouTube to understand what is already available and identifying gaps that you can fill with your unique perspective or approach. For instance, if you are interested in gaming, consider whether you will focus on game reviews, walkthroughs, competitive gaming strategies, or perhaps a mix of these elements tailored towards a specific game or genre.

- Assess your skills and strengths in relation to your passions.
- Analyze the competition by watching other YouTubers who share similar interests.
- Identify gaps in the market where your content could provide added value.

In addition to aligning with personal interests and skills, choosing the right niche also involves considering its potential for growth and engagement on YouTube. Some niches may be more saturated than others, making it harder for new channels to get noticed. However, with innovative ideas and a fresh take on popular topics, even crowded niches can offer opportunities for success.

Ultimately, discovering your passion and niche is an ongoing process that might evolve as you grow both personally and as a creator on YouTube. Embracing this journey with an open mind allows for flexibility in content creation while staying true to what excites you most.

2.2 Authenticity, Creativity, and Consistency

The journey from discovering your passion and niche to manifesting it into content creation on platforms like YouTube requires a harmonious blend of authenticity, creativity, and consistency. These three elements are not just strategies but the core principles that define the success and identity of a content creator.

Authenticity is about being true to oneself. It's the genuine expression of your thoughts, feelings, and perspectives in your content. Authenticity resonates with audiences because it builds trust. When viewers believe in the person behind the content, they're more likely to engage, subscribe, and follow their journey. Being authentic means sharing both successes and failures, allowing viewers to connect on a human level.

Creativity, on the other hand, is what sets your content apart from others in your niche. It's about how you present your passion in unique ways that captivate and entertain your audience. Creativity involves innovation—whether it's through storytelling techniques, video editing styles, or interactive formats—that keeps your content fresh and exciting. Remember, creativity is not just about what you create but how you think and approach problems or topics differently.

Consistency is crucial for growth on platforms like YouTube. It refers not only to posting regularly but also maintaining a consistent theme, quality, and voice across all your content. Consistency helps in building a loyal audience base as viewers know what to expect from your channel and when to expect it. This predictability fosters a sense of community among viewers who share similar interests.

- Identify what makes you unique and let that shine through every piece of content you create.
- Experiment with different formats or series within your niche to keep things interesting while staying true to yourself.
- Create a content calendar to plan out posts in advance; this helps in maintaining consistency without compromising on quality.

In conclusion, weaving together authenticity, creativity, and consistency can transform ordinary channels into extraordinary communities centered around shared passions. By staying true to oneself while continuously innovating and delivering reliable content, creators can forge deep connections with their audience that stand the test of time.

2.3 Understanding Your Audience

Understanding your audience is a pivotal step in the journey of content creation, acting as a bridge between the core principles of authenticity, creativity, and consistency, and their effective application. This understanding not only informs the creator about who they are communicating with but also shapes how they craft their messages to resonate on a deeper level. It's about recognizing the diverse needs, preferences, and challenges faced by your viewers and using this insight to tailor your content accordingly.

To truly connect with your audience, it's essential to delve into demographics such as age, location, and interests. However, going beyond these surface-level details to grasp the psychographics—values, attitudes, lifestyles—is what differentiates good content from great. This deeper dive enables creators to produce content that not only entertains but also educates, inspires, or solves problems for their audience.

Engagement metrics offer valuable insights into understanding your audience. Analyzing comments, likes/dislikes ratios, view durations, and sharing patterns can reveal what content resonates most strongly with your viewers. This feedback loop allows creators to refine their approach continually. For instance, if tutorial videos garner more engagement than vlogs on your channel, it signals a preference in your audience for educational over personal content.

- Conduct surveys or polls within your platform or social media channels to gather direct feedback from your audience about their preferences or content suggestions.

- Analyze demographic data provided by analytics tools on platforms like YouTube to understand who is watching your content.

- Monitor trends within comments and social media mentions to gauge sentiment and uncover emerging topics of interest among your viewers.

In conclusion, understanding your audience is an ongoing process that requires attention and adaptation. By leveraging both quantitative data (like analytics) and qualitative insights (such as direct feedback), creators can foster a stronger connection with their viewers. This alignment not only enhances viewer satisfaction but also supports sustained growth by ensuring that the content remains relevant and engaging over time.

3

Technical Foundations of a Successful Channel

3.1 Basics of Video Production and Editing

The foundation of any successful YouTube channel lies in mastering the basics of video production and editing. This skill set is crucial for teenage boys aspiring to make their mark on the platform, as it directly impacts the quality and engagement level of their content. Understanding the technical aspects of creating a video can transform a simple idea into a compelling story that captivates viewers.

Video production begins with pre-production planning, which includes brainstorming ideas, scripting, storyboard creation, and deciding on the filming locations. It's essential to have a clear vision of what you want to achieve with each video. This stage sets the direction for your project and ensures that you stay focused on your goals.

- Choosing the Right Equipment: While high-end cameras can produce superior video quality, they are not always necessary. Many successful YouTubers have started with just their smartphones. The key is understanding lighting and sound—two elements that can significantly enhance video quality even when using basic equipment.

- Filming Techniques: Learning basic filming techniques such as framing, composition, and camera angles can make a significant difference in visual storytelling. Experimenting with different shots adds dynamism to your videos, making them more engaging.

- Editing Essentials: Post-production is where your footage transforms into a polished video. Familiarity with editing software is vital; many free and paid options cater to beginners and advanced users alike. Editing allows you to cut out unnecessary parts, add music or effects, and ensure smooth transitions between scenes.

Beyond technical skills, creativity plays an indispensable role in video production and editing. It's about experimenting with different styles and techniques to find what best suits your message and resonates with your audience. Incorporating feedback from viewers can also guide improvements in content creation over time.

In conclusion, mastering the basics of video production and editing is not just about handling equipment or software; it's about crafting stories that engage and inspire your audience. With practice, patience, and persistence, any teenage boy can develop these skills to elevate his YouTube channel from ordinary to extraordinary.

3.2 SEO Strategies for Maximum Visibility

In the digital age, where content is king, understanding and implementing effective SEO (Search Engine Optimization) strategies are paramount for any YouTube channel aiming to achieve maximum visibility. SEO is not just about optimizing written content but also about making your video content discoverable to the right audience at the right time. This section delves into advanced techniques and strategies that go beyond basic keyword research, offering insights into how creators can enhance their channel's visibility and viewer engagement through strategic SEO practices.

The cornerstone of a robust SEO strategy for YouTube involves comprehensive keyword research tailored to video content. Identifying what your target audience is searching for allows you to craft titles, descriptions, and tags that align with those search queries, significantly increasing your chances of appearing in search results. However, the evolution of YouTube's algorithm demands a more nuanced approach than simply stuffing keywords into your video metadata.

Beyond these strategies, staying updated with YouTube's algorithm changes is crucial for adapting your SEO tactics effectively over time. Engaging with your community by responding to comments and incorporating viewer feedback into future content creation can also play a significant role in enhancing user experience and retention rates. Ultimately, combining these advanced SEO strategies with compelling video content is key to maximizing visibility and achieving long-term success on YouTube.

- User Engagement Signals: YouTube's algorithm places a high value on user engagement signals such as watch time, like-to-dislike ratio, comment activity, and the frequency of shares. Optimizing your content to boost these metrics can signal to YouTube that your videos are valuable to viewers, thus improving your rankings in search results and recommendations.

- Video Transcripts: Adding transcripts to your videos not only makes them accessible to a wider audience but also provides additional text for indexing by search engines. This can be particularly beneficial for long-tail keyword optimization, which targets more specific queries that are less competitive but highly relevant.

- Channel Authority: Building channel authority involves consistently producing high-quality content that garners positive user engagement. Over time, establishing yourself as a credible source on specific topics can lead to higher rankings across all your videos.

- Cross-Platform Promotion: Promoting your videos on social media platforms and embedding them in blog posts or websites can drive additional traffic and backlinks to your YouTube channel. These external signals contribute positively to both direct viewer engagement and indirect SEO benefits through increased visibility across different platforms.

3.3 Utilizing Analytics to Guide Content Strategy

In the realm of digital content creation, particularly on platforms like YouTube, leveraging analytics is not just beneficial; it's essential for crafting a successful content strategy. Analytics offer a treasure trove of data about how viewers interact with your content, providing insights that can significantly influence your creative decisions and strategic planning. This section explores how creators can effectively use analytics to refine their content strategy, ensuring their efforts resonate with their audience and align with platform algorithms.

Understanding viewer demographics is the first step in utilizing analytics effectively. Demographic information such as age, gender, location, and viewing device helps creators tailor their content to the specific preferences and needs of their audience. For instance, knowing that a significant portion of your audience watches videos on mobile devices could influence you to design your video thumbnails with mobile visibility in mind.

- Watch Time and Engagement Metrics: Watch time is a critical metric on YouTube, influencing how videos are recommended to users. Analyzing which videos hold viewers' attention longer can guide creators in producing more engaging content that matches or exceeds those performance benchmarks. Similarly, engagement metrics like likes, comments, and shares offer direct feedback from viewers about what they enjoy or don't enjoy about your content.

- Traffic Sources: Understanding where your viewers are coming from—be it search results, suggested videos, or external websites—can inform where to focus your promotional efforts and SEO strategies.

- Audience Retention: The Audience Retention graph provides insights into at what points viewers drop off from watching a video. This information is invaluable for identifying parts of your videos that may need improvement or elements that particularly captivate your audience.

Beyond these metrics, analyzing trends over time can uncover patterns in viewer behavior or preferences that might not be immediately apparent from individual videos. Seasonal trends, shifts in viewing habits, or changes in engagement levels can all signal when it's time to pivot your strategy or double down on what's working.

Incorporating viewer feedback gathered through comments into your analytics-driven strategy adds another layer of depth to understanding audience needs and desires. Engaging directly with viewers by asking for their input on future topics or formats not only boosts engagement but also makes them feel like an active part of the community you're building.

To sum up, utilizing analytics goes beyond mere number-crunching; it involves interpreting data within the context of broader viewer behavior trends and channel goals. By doing so diligently, creators can craft compelling content strategies that grow their channels organically and sustainably over time.

4

Engaging with Your Audience

4.1 Building a Community Around Your Channel

The essence of success on YouTube, especially for young creators like teenage boys, lies not just in the content they produce but significantly in the community they build around their channel. This community doesn't only represent an audience; it symbolizes a group of engaged individuals who share common interests, values, and a sense of belonging. Cultivating such a community requires more than just regular video uploads; it demands a strategic approach to interaction, content diversification, and creating spaces for engagement beyond YouTube itself.

Firstly, understanding your audience is crucial. This involves diving deep into analytics to grasp who your viewers are, what content they prefer, and when they are most active. Tailoring your content to meet these insights can significantly increase engagement rates. However, building a community goes beyond just analytics. It's about creating content that encourages interaction—asking questions, seeking opinions in comments, or even running polls or contests related to your niche.

Moreover, consistency in posting not only helps in keeping your channel active but also aids in setting expectations for your audience. When viewers know when to expect new content from you, it fosters a routine engagement that strengthens community bonds. Additionally, personal stories or behind-the-scenes glimpses into your life as a creator can add a layer of relatability and trust—key components of a strong community.

Incorporating these strategies effectively transforms passive viewers into active community members who are more likely to share your content across platforms. This not only amplifies your reach but also solidifies the loyalty of your audience base. Remember, the goal is not just growing numbers but nurturing an engaged and supportive community that grows with you over time.

- Engage directly with comments by replying thoughtfully to foster individual connections within your broader audience.
- Collaborate with other YouTubers to tap into new audiences and bring fresh perspectives to your channel.
- Create exclusive spaces like Discord servers or Facebook groups where your viewers can interact with each other and you on a more personal level.

In conclusion, building a vibrant community around your YouTube channel demands effort beyond content creationâ€"it requires genuine interaction and engagement strategies that resonate with your audience's preferences and behaviors. By focusing on these aspects diligently, young creators can establish not just successful channels but thriving communities that propel their growth on YouTube exponentially.

4.2 Effective Communication and Feedback Loops

Effective communication is the cornerstone of building and maintaining a strong community around any YouTube channel. It involves not only how you convey your message but also how you listen and respond to your audience. This two-way interaction fosters a sense of belonging among viewers, transforming them from passive consumers into active participants in your channel's ecosystem. The concept of feedback loops plays a crucial role in this process, serving as a mechanism for continuous improvement and deeper engagement.

At its core, effective communication on YouTube goes beyond the content of the videos themselves. It encompasses all forms of interaction with the audience, including comments, social media posts, live streams, and even the description boxes under each video. Each of these platforms offers unique opportunities for creators to connect with their viewers, understand their preferences, and tailor their content accordingly.

- Engaging directly with comments not only shows that you value viewer input but also encourages more people to share their thoughts and opinions.

- Utilizing social media platforms extends the conversation beyond YouTube, allowing for real-time interactions through stories, polls, or Q&A sessions.
- Live streaming can create a sense of immediacy and intimacy, offering an unfiltered glimpse into your creative process or daily life.

The feedback loop is initiated when creators actively seek out and reflect upon viewer responses to their content. This could be through analyzing comment trends, conducting surveys, or monitoring video performance metrics. By understanding what resonates with their audience—and what doesn't—creators can make informed decisions about future content directions, engagement strategies, and even branding choices.

However, effective communication is not just about gathering feedback; it's also about acting on it. Demonstrating that viewer input has influenced content creation not only validates their contribution but also deepens their investment in the channel's success. This reciprocal relationship between creator and community is what transforms casual viewers into loyal fans.

In conclusion, effective communication and feedback loops are vital for fostering an engaged community around a YouTube channel. By prioritizing these elements, creators can build lasting relationships with their audience that go beyond mere viewership numbers to cultivate a vibrant and supportive community.

4.3 Collaborations and Cross-Promotions

Collaborations and cross-promotions stand as pivotal strategies for amplifying audience engagement and expanding reach on platforms like YouTube. By partnering with other creators or brands, YouTubers can introduce their content to new audiences, infuse fresh perspectives into their videos, and create a synergy that benefits all parties involved. This strategy not only diversifies the content on the channel but also fosters a sense of community among creators.

Collaborations involve working with fellow content creators to produce joint content. This could range from guest appearances in each other's videos to co-creating a series that spans across both channels. The key to successful collaborations lies in choosing partners whose content aligns with your channel's theme and audience interests. This alignment ensures that the collaboration feels organic rather than forced, enhancing viewer reception and engagement.

- Identifying potential collaborators who share similar audience demographics or interests can maximize the impact of the partnership.
- Engaging in creative brainstorming sessions with collaborators can lead to innovative content ideas that captivate both audiences.
- Maintaining open communication and setting clear expectations from the outset are crucial for a smooth collaborative process.

Cross-promotions, on the other hand, involve leveraging different platforms or channels to promote content. This could include shoutouts on social media, featuring in newsletters of complementary brands, or even collaborating on promotional giveaways. Cross-promotions are particularly effective when they offer mutual benefits for all parties involvedâ€"be it through shared audiences, resources, or expertise.

In conclusion, collaborations and cross-promotions are powerful tools for YouTube creators aiming to expand their reach and engage more deeply with their audience. By carefully selecting partners and strategically planning these initiatives, creators can unlock new opportunities for growth while enriching their content offerings. The success of these endeavors hinges on authenticity, creativity, and mutual benefit—principles that resonate well with today's digital audiences.

- Utilizing social media platforms for teaser posts about upcoming collaborations can generate buzz and anticipation among followers.
- Partnering with brands for product placements or sponsored content can introduce your channel to new segments of your target market.
- Incorporating affiliate marketing links within video descriptions as part of a cross-promotion strategy can provide financial incentives alongside increased viewership.

5

Leveraging Social Media Platforms

5.1 Integrating Social Media into Your Growth Strategy

The digital age has transformed the way we consume content, making social media an indispensable tool for anyone looking to grow their presence online. For teenage boys aspiring to become influential YouTubers, integrating social media into their growth strategy is not just beneficial; it's essential. This approach leverages platforms beyond YouTube to amplify reach, engage with a broader audience, and create a multifaceted online persona that resonates with followers across different channels.

Understanding the synergy between YouTube and other social media platforms is the first step in crafting a cohesive growth strategy. Platforms like Instagram,

Twitter, and TikTok offer unique opportunities to showcase different aspects of your personality and content, creating a richer, more engaging brand image. For instance, Instagram can be used for behind-the-scenes photos or stories that provide a glimpse into your daily life or content creation process, making your YouTube persona more relatable and accessible.

Moreover, these platforms serve as vital tools for promoting new YouTube content. A well-timed tweet or Instagram story can drive significant traffic to your latest video, helping you capitalize on the algorithms of both YouTube and the social media platform you're using. The key is to understand the nuances of each platform's algorithm and user behavior to tailor your promotional strategies accordingly.

- Utilizing hashtags effectively to increase visibility on platforms like Instagram and Twitter.
- Engaging with followers through comments and direct messages to build a loyal community.
- Collaborating with other creators across social media platforms to tap into new audiences.

In addition to promotion and engagement, integrating social media into your growth strategy involves listening and adapting based on feedback from your audience across these channels. Social media provides immediate insights into what your audience enjoys through likes, comments, shares, and views. This real-time feedback loop allows you to refine your content strategy on YouTube and other platforms continuously.

To sum up, integrating social media into your growth strategy as an aspiring YouTuber involves much more than just cross-promotion of content. It requires a nuanced understanding of each platform's strengths, active engagement with your audience, and an adaptable content strategy that responds to feedback across all channels. By mastering these elements, teenage boys can significantly enhance their visibility online, attract a larger following, and build a powerful personal brand that spans multiple social media platforms.

5.2 Best Practices for Each Platform

The digital landscape is vast and varied, with each social media platform offering unique features and audiences. Understanding the best practices for each can significantly enhance your online presence and engagement. Here, we delve into strategies tailored to major platforms such as Instagram, Twitter, TikTok, and YouTube, providing insights beyond the initial summary's scope.

Instagram

Instagram thrives on visual content. High-quality photos and videos are paramount. Utilizing Instagram Stories and Reels can increase visibility and engagement, tapping into users' preferences for short-form content. Hashtags play a crucial role in discoverability, but they must be relevant to your niche. Engaging with your audience through comments, polls, and direct messages fosters a sense of community.

Twitter

Twitter is all about brevity and timeliness. Tweets that are concise yet impactful tend to perform better. It's essential to engage in trending topics relevant to your brand or persona while maintaining authenticity. Regular interaction with followers through replies and retweets builds relationships and keeps your audience engaged.

TikTok

TikTok favors creativity and trends. Participating in challenges, using trending sounds, and creating original content that resonates with users can lead to viral success. The platform's algorithm rewards engagement, so encouraging user interaction through comments or duets can amplify your reach.

YouTube

YouTube demands consistency in content quality and posting schedule. Videos should provide value—whether educational or entertaining—to encourage subscriptions and repeat views. Optimizing video titles, descriptions, and tags with keywords improves searchability while engaging with viewers through comments personalizes the experience.

- Consistency: Regular posting schedules help retain audience interest across platforms.
- Engagement: Interacting with followers creates a loyal community.

- Cross-Promotion: Leveraging multiple platforms can drive traffic between them.

In conclusion, mastering each social media platform's best practices allows for a more strategic approach to online growth. By tailoring content to fit the unique characteristics of each platform while maintaining a consistent brand voice and engaging directly with followers, creators can expand their reach effectively across the digital sphere.

5.3 Managing Multiple Platforms Efficiently

In the digital age, an effective social media strategy involves managing multiple platforms to maximize online presence and engagement. This approach, however, presents a unique set of challenges, including maintaining a consistent brand voice across diverse channels and efficiently allocating time and resources. Here, we explore strategies for streamlining this process, ensuring that efforts yield optimal results without overwhelming creators or marketers.

Firstly, understanding the distinct audience and content style of each platform is crucial. As outlined in the previous section, platforms like Instagram prioritize visual content while Twitter focuses on brevity and timeliness. Aligning your content strategy with these preferences ensures that your efforts resonate more effectively with each platform's user base.

Utilizing social media management tools is another key strategy for efficiency. Tools such as Hootsuite, Buffer, or Sprout Social allow users to schedule posts across multiple platforms from a single dashboard. This not only saves time but also provides valuable analytics to measure engagement and refine strategies accordingly.

- Content Calendar: Implementing a content calendar helps in planning and organizing posts in advance. This ensures a consistent posting schedule, which is vital for keeping your audience engaged across all platforms.

- Repurposing Content: Tailoring a single piece of content to suit different platforms can significantly reduce workload while maintaining an active presence everywhere. For example, a YouTube video can be edited into shorter clips for Instagram Reels or TikTok.

- Cross-Promotion: Leveraging each platform to promote content on others can drive cross-platform traffic and increase overall engagement without additional content creation efforts.

　Beyond these practical steps, fostering a community spirit through regular interaction with followers—such as responding to comments or featuring user-generated content—can encourage engagement across all platforms. While this requires dedication, it builds loyalty and amplifies word-of-mouth promotion.

　In conclusion, managing multiple social media platforms efficiently demands a strategic approach tailored to the unique characteristics of each site. By leveraging management tools, adopting a smart content strategy that includes repurposing and scheduling, and engaging directly with the online community, brands and creators can maximize their digital footprint without stretching their resources too thin.

6

Dealing with Criticism and Online Pressures

6.1 Handling Negative Comments Constructively

In the realm of YouTube and online content creation, encountering negative comments is an inevitable part of the journey. For teenage boys aspiring to grow their channels, learning how to handle such feedback constructively is crucial not only for personal development but also for channel growth. This section delves into strategies that can transform potentially disheartening experiences into opportunities for improvement and engagement.

Firstly, it's essential to differentiate between constructive criticism and outright negativity or trolling. Constructive criticism often comes with specific feedback that can help improve future content, whereas trolling lacks substance and is intended to provoke. Recognizing this difference enables creators to focus on comments that offer value, dismissing those meant to harm.

- Reflect on the Feedback: Take a moment to consider if there's a kernel of truth in the criticism. Sometimes, viewers may point out areas for improvement that the creator hasn't noticed.

- Engage Positively: Responding positively to constructive criticism can turn critics into supporters. Acknowledging their input shows maturity and openness to growth.

- Learn and Adapt: Use relevant feedback as a learning opportunity. Whether it's about video quality, content clarity, or presentation style, each piece of constructive criticism is a chance to evolve.

- Create a Supportive Community: Building a community around your channel that supports positive interaction can help mitigate the impact of negative comments. Encourage your audience to engage respectfully with each other.

Beyond dealing with individual comments, it's vital for young creators to cultivate resilience and maintain perspective. Not every critique is personal; often, they reflect the commenter's own preferences or issues rather than shortcomings in the content itself. Developing a thick skin allows creators to stay focused on their passion and goals without being derailed by negativity.

In conclusion, handling negative comments constructively is an invaluable skill in the digital age. It involves sifting through feedback for useful insights, engaging positively with your audience, and using criticism as fuel for growth rather than letting it hinder creativity. By adopting these strategies, teenage boys on YouTube can navigate online pressures more effectively, fostering both personal development and channel success.

6.2 Balancing School, Life, and YouTube

For many young creators, juggling the demands of school, personal life, and a burgeoning YouTube channel presents a formidable challenge. This balancing act requires not only time management skills but also an understanding of priorities and self-care. The key to success lies in finding harmony between these aspects of life, ensuring that none is neglected at the expense of others.

Firstly, setting a realistic schedule that allocates specific times for content creation alongside academic responsibilities is crucial. This might mean dedicating weekends or certain evenings to filming and editing, ensuring that schoolwork is not compromised. It's important for young YouTubers to remember that while their channel is significant, education provides a foundation for future opportunities.

- Establish Clear Priorities: Understanding what needs immediate attention and what can wait is essential. Sometimes, this may mean taking a short break from YouTube during exam periods or critical school projects.

- Maintain Flexibility: While having a schedule is important, being too rigid can lead to burnout. It's vital to stay adaptable and adjust plans as needed based on workload and personal well-being.

- Embrace Efficiency: Learning to work efficiently can save precious time. This includes batching content creation tasks together or using school projects as content material when appropriate.

- Create Boundaries: Setting boundaries with online activities ensures that there's time left for offline relationships and self-care. Engaging in hobbies outside YouTube helps maintain mental health and creativity.

Beyond these strategies, it's beneficial for young creators to communicate openly with family and friends about their goals and challenges. Support from loved ones can provide motivation and assistance during busy periods or when feeling overwhelmed. Additionally, connecting with fellow YouTubers who face similar struggles offers valuable insights and camaraderie.

In conclusion, balancing school, life, and YouTube is an ongoing process that requires mindfulness about one's limits and needs. By prioritizing effectively, staying flexible in planning, working efficiently, setting boundaries for work-life balance, seeking support from others, young creators can navigate the complexities of managing multiple responsibilities while pursuing their passion for content creation on YouTube.

6.3 Maintaining Mental Health in the Digital Space

In an era where digital presence is nearly as significant as physical existence, maintaining mental health online has become a critical challenge, especially for content creators and young individuals navigating the complexities of social media and digital platforms. The pressures of constant connectivity, comparison, and public scrutiny can take a toll on one's psychological well-being. This section delves into strategies for safeguarding mental health in the digital realm, ensuring that individuals can thrive both online and offline.

The first step towards maintaining mental health online is recognizing the unique challenges posed by digital spaces. These include the blurring of public and private life boundaries, cyberbullying, and the phenomenon of social comparison exacerbated by curated portrayals of success and happiness on social media platforms. Acknowledging these factors is crucial in developing effective coping mechanisms.

- Digital Detox: Periodically disconnecting from digital devices allows individuals to recharge mentally and fosters mindfulness. Designating tech-free times or zones encourages engagement with the physical world, enhancing personal relationships and reducing stress.

- Curate Your Feed: Actively managing social media feeds to include positive influences while minimizing exposure to toxic or distressing content can significantly improve one's mood and outlook.

- Engage in Positive Online Communities: Participating in supportive online groups or forums that share one's interests or values can provide a sense of belonging and support, counteracting feelings of isolation or inadequacy.

- Mindful Consumption: Being aware of how much time is spent on various platforms and what content is consumed helps in identifying patterns that may be harmful to mental health. This awareness enables more intentional use of technology.

Beyond individual strategies, seeking professional help when overwhelmed by negative emotions related to online experiences is vital. Therapists specializing in digital wellness can offer tailored advice for navigating online challenges while preserving mental health. Additionally, leveraging privacy settings to control who can interact with you online and being selective about what personal information is shared publicly are practical steps toward creating a safer digital environment.

In conclusion, while the digital space offers unparalleled opportunities for connection, creativity, and learning, it also presents new challenges for mental health. By adopting mindful practices such as digital detoxes, curating feeds, engaging with positive communities, practicing mindful consumption, utilizing privacy controls effectively, and seeking professional guidance when necessary, individuals can protect their mental well-being in an increasingly connected world.

7

Monetization Strategies

7.1 Understanding YouTube's Monetization Policies

The digital landscape offers a plethora of opportunities for young creators to showcase their talents and passions. Among these platforms, YouTube stands out as a beacon for aspiring content creators, especially teenage boys looking to make their mark in the world of online entertainment and information dissemination. However, navigating the monetization aspect of YouTube can be as challenging as it is crucial. Understanding YouTube's monetization policies is the first step towards turning a passion project into a potential source of income.

YouTube's Partner Program (YPP) is at the heart of its monetization model. To be eligible for this program, creators must meet specific criteria such as accumulating over 1,000 subscribers and achieving 4,000 watch hours over the last 12 months. These thresholds are designed to ensure that only dedicated and consistent creators can monetize their content. This policy underscores the importance of building a solid subscriber base and creating engaging content that keeps viewers coming back for more.

Once part of YPP, creators have access to various revenue streams including ad revenue, channel memberships, super chat features in live streams, and merchandise shelves. Each of these avenues comes with its own set of rules and best practices. For instance, ad revenue depends on not just the number of views but also on adhering to YouTube's advertiser-friendly content guidelines. This means that videos containing explicit material or controversial subjects may be deemed ineligible for monetization.

Beyond understanding these policies and revenue options, successful YouTubers must also navigate copyright laws carefully. Copyright strikes can not only lead to demonetization but also potentially result in channel termination. Thus, it's imperative for creators to use original content or obtain proper licenses when incorporating third-party materials into their videos.

- Ad Revenue: Creators earn money through ads displayed on their videos.
- Channel Memberships: Viewers pay monthly subscriptions for exclusive perks.
- Super Chat: Fans pay to highlight their messages during live streams.
- Merchandise Shelf: Creators sell branded merchandise directly through YouTube.

In conclusion, while YouTube offers an incredible platform for young creators to share their passions with the world, understanding and navigating its monetization policies is key to turning those creative endeavors into sustainable ventures. By familiarizing themselves with YPP requirements, exploring different revenue streams wisely, and respecting copyright laws, teenage boys can lay down a strong foundation for success in the dynamic world of YouTube content creation.

7.2 Diversifying Income Streams as a Creator

In the dynamic world of content creation, relying on a single income source can be precarious. Diversifying income streams not only enhances financial stability but also opens up new avenues for creative expression and audience engagement. For creators, especially those navigating platforms like YouTube, diversification is not just a strategy but a necessity in the face of ever-changing algorithms and monetization policies.

The essence of diversification lies in tapping into multiple revenue channels. While ad revenue might be the most direct form of income for many YouTubers, it's subject to fluctuations based on viewer preferences, advertiser demands, and platform regulations. Expanding beyond this singular source can mitigate risks associated with these variables.

- Affiliate Marketing: Creators can earn commissions by promoting products or services and including affiliate links in their video descriptions. This method aligns well with content that naturally incorporates product reviews or recommendations.

- Patreon and Crowdfunding: Platforms like Patreon allow creators to receive funding directly from their audience in exchange for exclusive content or perks. Crowdfunding campaigns can also support specific projects or endeavors.

- Sponsored Content: Collaborating with brands on sponsored videos introduces another lucrative stream. It requires building a strong personal brand and maintaining authenticity to ensure audience trust.

- Digital Products and Courses: Creators with expertise in particular areas can develop digital products such as e-books, courses, or downloadable assets. This approach leverages their knowledge base to generate income while providing value to their audience.

Beyond these methods, exploring unconventional paths like hosting live events (virtual or physical), offering consulting services, or even creating original merchandise can further diversify income sources. Each avenue requires understanding the target audience's needs and preferences to offer relevant and compelling value propositions.

In conclusion, diversifying income streams empowers creators to build sustainable careers by reducing dependency on any single source of revenue. It encourages innovation and adaptability—qualities essential for long-term success in the ever-evolving landscape of content creation. By strategically exploring various monetization methods, creators can ensure financial stability while continuing to engage their audiences through compelling content.

7.3 Brand Partnerships and Sponsorships

In the realm of content creation, brand partnerships and sponsorships stand out as a pivotal monetization strategy that goes beyond traditional advertising or affiliate marketing. This approach involves creators collaborating directly with brands to produce content that promotes a product, service, or message. Unlike other revenue streams, this method requires a delicate balance between maintaining audience trust and meeting the brand's objectives.

The essence of successful brand partnerships lies in alignment—finding brands whose values, audience, and products resonate with those of the creator. This synergy not only ensures authenticity in promotion but also enhances the likelihood of audience acceptance and engagement. Creators often leverage their unique voice and platform to introduce their followers to products or services in a manner that feels natural and unobtrusive.

- Identifying Compatible Brands: The process begins with identifying brands that share similar values and have potential appeal to the creator's audience. This compatibility is crucial for authentic endorsements.

- Negotiating Terms: Once a compatible brand is identified, negotiating terms that benefit both parties while ensuring creative freedom is essential. Clear communication about expectations and deliverables can set the foundation for a successful partnership.

- Creating Authentic Content: The core of these partnerships is producing content that seamlessly integrates the sponsored product or service while retaining the creator's voice and style. Authenticity is key; audiences are more receptive when they believe in the genuineness of the endorsement.

Moreover, navigating these partnerships requires transparency with one's audience about sponsored content to maintain trust—a practice mandated by many regulatory bodies worldwide. Successful creators disclose sponsorships clearly and concisely, ensuring their audience understands when content is sponsored.

In conclusion, brand partnerships and sponsorships offer creators an avenue to diversify their income while providing value to both their audience and partnering brands. When executed thoughtfully, these collaborations can enhance a creator's content offering without compromising integrity or audience trust. As such, they represent not just a monetization strategy but an opportunity for creative collaboration and growth.

8

Advanced Content Creation Techniques

8.1 Storytelling and Visual Narratives

In the realm of digital content creation, particularly on platforms like YouTube, storytelling and visual narratives stand as pivotal elements that can significantly enhance a creator's connection with their audience. This approach transcends mere information sharing, inviting viewers into a meticulously crafted world where every video serves as a chapter in a broader narrative. For teenage boys aspiring to grow their YouTube channels, mastering the art of storytelling and visual narratives is not just an advantage; it's a necessity.

At its core, effective storytelling on YouTube involves weaving personal experiences, insights, and creativity into content that resonates with viewers on an emotional level. It's about transforming ordinary videos into compelling stories that captivate and engage. This requires a deep understanding of narrative structures—knowing how to set up a premise, introduce conflict or challenges, and guide the audience through to resolution or reflection.

Visual narratives complement storytelling by enhancing the way stories are told through imagery, cinematography, and editing techniques. The use of visuals is not merely decorative but serves to amplify the impact of the story being told. For instance, strategic camera angles can emphasize emotions or highlight key moments, while thoughtful editing can pace the narrative for maximum effect.

Beyond individual videos, developing a cohesive channel theme or storyline can encourage viewers to follow along on your journey, eagerly anticipating each new installment. This long-term engagement is crucial for building a dedicated subscriber base.

- Understanding your audience: Crafting stories that resonate begins with knowing who you're speaking to. This involves identifying common interests, challenges, and aspirations shared by your target demographic.

- Authenticity: Genuine stories have the power to connect deeply with viewers. Sharing real experiences or lessons learned can foster trust and loyalty among your audience.
- Creative presentation: Experimenting with different visual styles or storytelling techniques can help distinguish your content in a crowded space.

In conclusion, storytelling and visual narratives are not just tools for entertainment but powerful strategies for growth on YouTube. They enable creators to forge meaningful connections with their audience, turning casual viewers into committed fans. As young creators navigate their path on YouTube, embracing these techniques will be instrumental in crafting content that stands out for its depth, creativity, and emotional resonance.

8.2 Advanced Editing Techniques for Engagement

In the digital age, where content is king, advanced editing techniques stand as the queen, orchestrating engagement and captivating audiences. The art of editing transcends basic cuts and transitions; it's about creating a rhythm that pulses through your content, making every second count towards retaining viewer interest. This section delves into sophisticated editing strategies that can elevate your videos from good to unforgettable, ensuring they not only grab attention but hold it tight until the very end.

Dynamic pacing is the heartbeat of engaging content. It involves varying the speed and rhythm of your video to match the emotional intensity of the story you're telling. Fast cuts can inject energy and excitement, while slower moments allow for reflection and deeper connection. The key is balanceâ€"knowing when to ramp up the pace to keep viewers on their toes and when to slow down to let them breathe.

- Color grading plays a pivotal role in setting the tone and mood of your video. Beyond correcting footage, color grading allows you to stylize your visuals, evoking specific emotions or atmospheres that align with your narrative.
- Sound design is often an underutilized tool in video editing. Strategic use of music, sound effects, and

silence can dramatically enhance storytelling, guiding viewers' emotions and expectations subtly yet powerfully.

- Visual effects (VFX) offer endless possibilities to add flair or communicate complex ideas quickly. Whether it's simple text animations or more elaborate composites, VFX can make your content stand out in a crowded digital landscape.

Engagement also hinges on relatability and immersion. Techniques like breaking the fourth wall with direct addresses or incorporating viewer-generated content can foster a sense of community and participation among your audience. Moreover, leveraging analytics tools to understand viewer preferences can inform more targeted editing choices, tailoring content that resonates deeply with your demographic.

In conclusion, advanced editing techniques are not just about polishing visuals but are instrumental in crafting experiences that engage viewers emotionally and intellectually. By mastering these skills, creators can transform passive viewers into active participants who are not only more likely to watch videos in their entirety but also more inclined to return for future content.

8.3 Innovating with Trends While Staying True to Your Niche

In the ever-evolving landscape of content creation, striking a balance between innovating with trends and staying true to your niche is both an art and a science. This delicate equilibrium ensures that your content remains relevant and engaging, without alienating your core audience. The key lies in understanding the essence of your niche while being open to integrating new trends that complement rather than overshadow it.

One effective strategy is to monitor emerging trends within and adjacent to your niche. This proactive approach allows you to identify which trends have the potential to resonate with your audience before they become mainstream. However, not all trends will align with your brand's identity or values, making discernment crucial. Selecting trends that enhance your message rather than dilute it can invigorate your content strategy, offering fresh perspectives to your audience while reinforcing your expertise and authenticity.

- Collaboration with influencers or thought leaders who embody these trends can introduce them credibly within your niche. This not only lends authority but also facilitates a smoother integration of new ideas into familiar contexts.

- Utilizing data analytics tools can provide insights into how similar trends have performed within your niche historically, guiding more informed decisions about which innovations are worth pursuing.

- Engaging directly with your community through polls or discussions about emerging trends can foster a sense of participation and investment in the evolution of your content, ensuring that innovation feels inclusive rather than imposed.

Incorporating new trends should always aim to add value for the audience, whether by educating, entertaining, or inspiring them in novel ways that still feel inherently 'you'. By maintaining this focus on delivering value, you safeguard against chasing trends for their own sake—a practice that can quickly lead to content feeling disjointed or insincere.

In conclusion, navigating the dynamic interplay between trend innovation and niche fidelity requires a blend of vigilance, creativity, and strategic thinking. By carefully selecting trends that amplify rather than alter the core appeal of your content, you can continue to captivate and grow your audience amidst an ever-changing digital landscape.

9

Growing Beyond YouTube

9.1 Expanding Your Brand to Other Mediums

The digital landscape is vast and ever-evolving, offering a plethora of platforms beyond YouTube where creative content can thrive. For teenage boys embarking on their journey to become influential content creators, understanding the importance of diversifying their presence across various mediums is crucial. This expansion not only amplifies their reach but also safeguards their brand against the unpredictability of platform-specific changes or challenges.

One fundamental approach to expanding a brand beyond YouTube involves identifying and leveraging other social media platforms where potential audiences spend their time. Platforms like Instagram, TikTok, and Twitter offer unique formats for storytelling and engagement, allowing creators to showcase different facets of their personality and content. For instance, Instagram's visual-centric nature is perfect for behind-the-scenes photos or short video clips that complement longer YouTube videos, while TikTok's format can be used to create viral challenges or snippets related to your main content.

Another significant avenue for brand expansion is through podcasting. Podcasts have surged in popularity and offer an intimate way to connect with audiences through in-depth discussions, interviews, or solo episodes exploring topics of interest. This medium allows creators to dive deeper into subjects they're passionate about without worrying about the visual elements required for YouTube videos.

Blogging or writing articles on platforms like Medium can also enhance a creator's visibility. Written content allows for detailed explorations of topics that might only be briefly covered in videos. It also improves search engine visibility, making it easier for new audiences to discover you online.

- Utilizing Instagram Stories and IGTV for real-time engagement and longer-form content respectively.

- Leveraging TikTok's algorithm favoring creative and original content to gain rapid visibility.
- Starting a podcast as a complementary medium to discuss topics in depth or share personal stories.
- Writing detailed blog posts or articles that provide additional value and context around video content.

In conclusion, expanding your brand across multiple mediums not only increases your reach but also provides your audience with diverse ways to interact with your content. Each platform offers unique advantages and caters to different audience preferences, enabling creators to build a more resilient and multifaceted online presence. By strategically choosing which mediums best align with their brand identity and goals, young YouTubers can significantly enhance their influence beyond the confines of a single platform.

9.2 Engaging with Fans Off-YouTube

Engaging with fans beyond the confines of YouTube is a pivotal strategy for content creators aiming to solidify their brand and foster a deeper connection with their audience. This engagement not only enriches the fan experience but also creates a more robust community around the creator's content, extending their influence and reach. Platforms such as Instagram, Twitter, and Facebook allow for real-time interaction, while other mediums like podcasts and blogs offer avenues for more in-depth exploration of topics that resonate with both the creator and their audience.

One effective method for engaging with fans off-YouTube is through hosting live Q&A sessions on social media platforms. These sessions can provide an intimate setting for creators to answer questions directly from fans, share insights into their creative process, and discuss upcoming projects or ideas. The immediacy of live interaction significantly enhances the sense of community and personal connection between creators and their audience.

- Utilizing Instagram Live or Twitter Spaces to host regular Q&A sessions or discussions.

- Creating exclusive content for Patreon supporters, offering them behind-the-scenes access or early previews of upcoming work.

- Launching a Discord server or Facebook group where fans can gather to discuss content, share ideas, and interact directly with the creator.
- Organizing virtual meetups or webinars on platforms like Zoom to engage with fans on a more personal level.

Beyond digital interactions, creators can also explore offline engagements such as fan meet-ups, workshops, or participation in conventions related to their niche. These events provide tangible opportunities for fans to connect with creators face-to-face, further strengthening the bond within the community. Additionally, leveraging email newsletters as a means of keeping fans informed about new content, events, or merchandise releases ensures that audiences remain engaged across multiple touchpoints.

In conclusion, engaging with fans off-YouTube requires a multifaceted approach that leverages both online and offline channels. By creating varied opportunities for interaction beyond video comments or likes, creators can build stronger relationships with their audience. This not only enhances fan loyalty but also contributes significantly to building a sustainable brand presence across different platforms.

9.3 Long-term Brand Building Strategies

The essence of long-term brand building for content creators extends far beyond the immediate gratification of likes and views. It involves a strategic approach to establishing a brand that resonates with audiences over time, ensuring sustainability and growth in an ever-evolving digital landscape. This strategy is pivotal for creators who aim to transition from being seen as mere content providers to becoming influential brand owners with loyal communities.

One foundational aspect of long-term brand building is consistency in content quality and messaging. This consistency helps in reinforcing the creator's brand identity, making it easier for audiences to recognize and connect with the brand across various platforms. Moreover, it establishes a level of trust and reliability among the audience, which is crucial for sustaining engagement over time.

- Developing a unique visual style and tone of voice that are consistent across all content and platforms.

- Creating a content calendar to maintain regular posting schedules, ensuring ongoing engagement with the audience.
- Investing in high-quality production values to enhance the viewer's experience and reinforce the brand's commitment to excellence.

In addition to consistency, diversifying content offerings plays a significant role in long-term brand building. By exploring different formats and platforms, creators can reach wider audiences and tap into new markets. This diversification not only helps in mitigating risks associated with platform-specific changes but also enriches the creator's portfolio, showcasing their versatility and adaptability.

- Expanding into podcasting or blogging to delve deeper into topics of interest, offering value beyond entertainment.
- Leveraging emerging platforms and technologies (e.g., virtual reality experiences) to stay ahead of trends and capture new audience segments.

Furthermore, community building is at the heart of sustainable brand growth. Engaging with fans through personalized interactions fosters a sense of belonging among the audience, transforming passive viewers into active community members who contribute ideas, feedback, and support for the creator's endeavors.

- Implementing loyalty programs or exclusive membership perks for dedicated fans to deepen their connection with the brand.
- Encouraging user-generated content campaigns that allow fans to be part of the creative process, enhancing community engagement.

Last but not least, strategic collaborations with other creators or brands can significantly amplify a creator's reach while adding value through complementary strengths. These partnerships should be chosen carefully to ensure alignment with the creator's brand values and audience interests, thereby fostering organic growth through shared communities.

- Partnering on cross-promotional projects that introduce each partner's audience to new but relevant content experiences.

- Engaging in social causes or community initiatives that resonate with both partners' brands, enhancing credibility and social impact.

In conclusion, long-term brand building requires a multifaceted approach that emphasizes quality consistency, diversification of content offerings, active community engagement, and strategic partnerships. By focusing on these areas, creators can establish enduring brands that thrive amidst changing digital trends and maintain meaningful connections with their audiences over time.

10

Interviews with Successful YouTubers

10.1 Lessons from Their Journeys

The path to becoming a successful YouTuber, especially for teenage boys, is filled with unique challenges and invaluable lessons. The insights gained from those who have navigated this journey successfully are not just motivational stories but also practical guides that can help shape the future of aspiring creators. Understanding these lessons is crucial in developing a mindset that appreciates the value of persistence, innovation, and authenticity in the digital content creation space.

One of the first lessons learned from successful YouTubers is the importance of **authenticity**. In an online world brimming with content, what sets one apart is their ability to stay true to themselves while connecting with their audience. This authenticity fosters trust and loyalty among viewers, which is indispensable in building a community around your channel.

Another critical lesson is the significance of **consistency**. Not just in terms of uploading videos on a regular schedule but also in maintaining the quality and thematic focus of the content. Consistency helps in establishing a brand identity for your channel and aids algorithms in understanding how to recommend your content effectively.

Beyond these strategic insights, managing criticism constructively without letting it deter one's passion is vital for mental health and sustained growth. Balancing educational commitments with YouTube pursuits requires effective time management skills—a challenge that many young creators learn to navigate early on.

- Creativity and innovation are pivotal. The digital landscape is ever-evolving, and so are viewer preferences. Successful YouTubers emphasize staying ahead by experimenting with new formats, exploring trends early, and always looking for ways to improve their content.

- Leveraging analytics plays a crucial role in growth. Understanding which videos perform well, why they do so, and who watches them can inform future content strategies that align more closely with audience preferences.

- Engagement beyond YouTube. Building a presence on other social media platforms can amplify reach and create additional touchpoints for engaging with fans. It's about creating a community around your brand across multiple platforms.

In conclusion, these journeys underscore that success on YouTube goes beyond mere talent or luck; it's about hard work, learning from failures, adapting to changes, and above all, believing in one's vision. Aspiring YouTubers should take these lessons to heart as they embark on their own paths towards creating impactful online presences.

10.2 Diverse Paths to Success

The journey to becoming a successful YouTuber is as varied as the creators themselves. While lessons on authenticity, consistency, creativity, leveraging analytics, and engagement beyond YouTube form the bedrock of success in the digital content realm, the routes taken to achieve prominence highlight the individuality of each creator's path. This diversity not only illustrates the myriad ways success can be attained but also underscores that there is no one-size-fits-all approach in the world of content creation.

For some, success comes from tapping into niche markets with dedicated audiences eager for content specific to their interests. These creators often find that by serving a smaller segment of viewers exceptionally well, they can build a loyal community around their channel. This approach contrasts with those who aim for broader appeal, creating content that resonates with a wide audience by covering trending topics or engaging in popular challenges.

Another path involves collaboration and networking with other creators. By leveraging each other's audiences, YouTubers can experience mutual growth and reach new viewers who might otherwise remain unaware of their content. This strategy emphasizes the importance of community over competition and showcases how relationships within the platform can lead to significant opportunities for exposure and success.

In conclusion, while foundational principles provide guidance for aspiring YouTubers, it's clear that success on this platform can come from many directions. The stories of successful creators reveal an ecosystem rich with opportunity for those willing to explore new ideas, adapt to change, and most importantly, engage authentically with their audience. As such, understanding these diverse paths offers both inspiration and practical insight for anyone looking to carve out their own space on YouTube.

- Innovation in content delivery also marks a distinct route to success. Some creators experiment with unique formats or storytelling techniques that set them apart from others in their genre. Whether it's through interactive videos, blending different types of media, or utilizing cutting-edge technology like virtual reality, these innovators push the boundaries of what's possible on YouTube.
- Persistence and adaptation are key themes among successful YouTubers who have weathered changes in

platform algorithms, shifting viewer preferences, and even global events affecting video production and consumption habits. Their ability to pivot strategies while maintaining their core identity has been crucial in sustaining long-term growth.

- Engaging deeply with their audience, beyond just responding to comments or messages. Successful creators often host live streams, participate in Q&A sessions, or create content based directly on viewer feedback. This level of interaction fosters a strong sense of community and belonging among viewers, further cementing loyalty to the channel.

10.3 Advice for Upcoming Creators

The journey to becoming a successful YouTuber is filled with challenges, learning curves, and the constant need for adaptation. Drawing from the experiences of established creators, this section delves into practical advice aimed at those embarking on their content creation journey. The insights provided here are designed to guide upcoming creators through the initial stages of channel growth, content strategy development, and audience engagement.

First and foremost, understanding your audience is crucial. Successful YouTubers emphasize the importance of knowing who you are creating content for and what needs or interests your videos fulfill. This connection with your audience lays the foundation for building a loyal community around your channel.

- Consistency is key. Regularly uploading content keeps your audience engaged and helps establish a routine that viewers can look forward to. It's not just about quantity; consistency also refers to maintaining a standard of quality that meets or exceeds viewer expectations.

- Authenticity cannot be overstated. Viewers are drawn to creators who are genuine and transparent in their communication. Authenticity fosters trust and relatability, which in turn strengthens viewer loyalty.

- Leverage analytics. YouTube provides a wealth of data through its analytics platform. Successful creators use this information to understand viewer behavior, identify what works (and what doesn’t), and tailor their content strategy accordingly.

- Engagement goes beyond video uploads. Interacting with your audience through comments, social media, or live streams adds a personal touch that can significantly enhance viewer loyalty. It shows that you value their support and feedback.

In addition to these foundational principles, it's important for new creators to experiment with different types of content and formats until they find what resonates most with their audience. Innovation should not be feared; it should be embraced as an opportunity for differentiation and growth.

Persistence plays a critical role in the path to success on YouTube. The platform's landscape is constantly evolving, as are viewer preferences and behaviors. Successful YouTubers adapt to these changes without losing sight of their core identity or values. They understand that setbacks are part of the process and use them as learning opportunities rather than reasons to give up.

In conclusion, while there is no one-size-fits-all blueprint for success on YouTube, certain practices have proven effective across diverse channels and niches. By focusing on authenticity, consistency, engagement, analytics-driven decision making, experimentation with content formats, and persistence in the face of challenges, upcoming creators can set themselves on a path toward building a successful YouTube channel.

11

Practical Exercises for Aspiring YouTubers

1.1 Identifying Your Unique Selling Proposition (USP)

In the vast and ever-expanding universe of YouTube, standing out is both an art and a science. For teenage boys embarking on their journey to become influential content creators, identifying and leveraging their Unique Selling Proposition (USP) is crucial. This concept isn't just a marketing buzzword; it's the essence of what makes your channel different and more appealing to your target audience compared to countless others.

Your USP is the intersection of your passions, skills, and the unique perspective you bring to your content. It answers the question, "Why should someone watch my videos instead of others?" This could be anything from a distinctive editing style, an unusual talent, or even a new approach to common topics. The key is to delve deep into what you love doing and how you can do it differently from anyone else on the platform.

- Passion meets niche: Start by listing down what you're most passionate about. Then research how these interests are currently represented on YouTube. Is there a gap you can fill? Can you approach this niche from a fresh angle?

- Skills that set you apart: Consider your skills, both in terms of content creation (like storytelling or video editing) and any other talents that could enhance your videos (such as playing an instrument or performing magic tricks). How can these skills contribute to making your content unique?

- Your personality as a brand: Never underestimate the power of personality. Sometimes, it's not just about what you present but how you present it. Your humor, sincerity, enthusiasm, or even sarcasm could be what draws viewers to your channel.

Finding your USP requires introspection, experimentation, and feedback. It's about combining what you're good at with what you enjoy doing in such a way that provides value or entertainment that isn't readily available elsewhere on YouTube. Remember, authenticity plays a significant role in this process; viewers are drawn to creators who are genuine and relatable.

Once identified, your USP should inform every aspect of your channelâ€"from the content itself to how you market it on social media platforms. It becomes part of your brand identity, helping potential subscribers quickly understand who you are and why they should care. Embracing and consistently delivering on your USP will not only help attract viewers but also build a loyal community around your channel.

11.2 Creating an Engaging First Video

The journey of a thousand miles begins with a single step, and in the world of YouTube, that first step is your debut video. Crafting an engaging first video is paramount as it sets the tone for your channel and gives viewers a taste of what to expect. This initial offering is your opportunity to hook your audience, showcase your unique selling proposition (USP), and differentiate yourself from the sea of content creators.

First impressions matter immensely on YouTube. Your debut needs to be more than just informative or entertaining; it should resonate with your target audience on a personal level. This connection can be achieved by weaving elements of your personality into the content, whether through humor, storytelling, or sharing personal anecdotes. Remember, authenticity fosters engagement and loyalty among viewers.

- Focus on Quality Over Quantity: Your first video doesn't have to be long, but it does need to be high-quality. Invest time in learning basic video editing skills to ensure your video looks polished and professional.

- Introduce Yourself: Start by introducing yourself and explaining the purpose of your channel. Share why you are passionate about your niche and what viewers can gain by subscribing to your channel.

- Showcase Your USP: Clearly highlight what sets you apart from other YouTubers in your niche. Whether it's a unique format, perspective, or presentation style, make sure it shines through in your first video.

Incorporating feedback is also crucial at this stage. After publishing your first video, engage with any comments you receive and take note of viewer suggestions for future content. This not only helps in refining your approach but also builds a community around your channel from day one.

To sum up, creating an engaging first video involves a blend of showcasing high-quality content that highlights your USP while being authentic and relatable to your audience. It's about making a memorable entrance into the YouTube community that paves the way for growth and success.

11.3 Developing a Content Calendar

After establishing a strong start with an engaging first video, the next crucial step for aspiring YouTubers is to develop a content calendar. This strategic tool is essential for planning and organizing future content in a way that ensures consistency, which is key to building and maintaining an audience on YouTube. A well-thought-out content calendar not only helps in managing your workflow but also in aligning your videos with audience expectations and special events or trends.

Consistency in posting schedules helps viewers know when to expect new content, fostering a habit of watching your channel. However, consistency doesn't mean sacrificing quality for quantity. The balance between the two is what retains audience interest over time. A content calendar aids in this by allowing you to plan ahead, ensuring that you have ample time to create high-quality content without feeling rushed.

- Identify Key Themes: Start by identifying themes or topics that resonate with your target audience and are central to your channel's niche. This thematic approach ensures your content remains focused and relevant.

- Plan for Seasonality: Take advantage of seasonal trends or holidays that align with your channel's theme. Planning content around these times can attract more viewers looking for related content.

- Incorporate Series: Creating series within your channel can keep viewers coming back for more. Use your content calendar to plan these series effectively, spacing them out in a way that keeps interest alive.

Beyond just scheduling videos, a content calendar should also include time allocated for scriptwriting, filming, editing, and promoting each video across social media platforms. This comprehensive approach ensures each aspect of the video creation process is given due attention, enhancing the overall quality of your output.

In conclusion, developing a content calendar is more than just plotting dates on a calendar; it's about strategically planning your creative process to maximize engagement with your audience while maintaining a manageable workflow for yourself. By doing so, you set up both yourself and your channel for long-term success on YouTube.

12

Conclusion - Embarking on Your YouTube Journey

12.1 Recapitulating Key Learnings

The journey of becoming a successful YouTuber, especially for teenage boys, is filled with unique challenges and opportunities that require not just creativity and passion but also strategic thinking and resilience. This section revisits the essential lessons outlined in the book, emphasizing their importance in navigating the digital landscape of YouTube content creation.

Firstly, understanding one's identity and staying true to it while creating content is paramount. Authenticity resonates with audiences more than anything else. It's about finding a balance between what you love to create and what your audience loves to watch. This alignment of passion and audience interest forms the foundation of a successful YouTube channel.

Secondly, consistency cannot be overlooked. The digital space is inundated with content, making visibility a challenge for many creators. Regular posting schedules and maintaining quality over quantity ensure that your channel remains relevant and engaging to your audience. Consistency also aids in algorithmic favorability on YouTube, increasing the chances of your content being recommended to potential subscribers.

- Leveraging SEO strategies effectively to enhance discoverability.
- Understanding analytics to refine content strategy based on performance data.
- Utilizing social media platforms for cross-promotion and community building.

Beyond technical skills, addressing the psychological aspects of being a young creator is crucial. Dealing with criticism constructively and managing time efficiently between academic responsibilities and content creation are vital skills that support sustainable growth on YouTube without compromising mental health or educational commitments.

Inspiration drawn from interviews with successful YouTubers who began their journeys as teenagers underscores the diversity of paths available to achieve success on this platform. These stories highlight that perseverance, learning from failures, and adapting strategies based on feedback are key components of growth.

Finally, practical exercises provided throughout the book encourage direct application of learned concepts. These activities not only solidify theoretical knowledge but also foster hands-on experience in channel development—from identifying niches to crafting engaging videos—ensuring readers are well-equipped to embark on their YouTube journey with confidence.

In conclusion, "How To Grow On YouTube As A Teenage Boy" serves as more than just a guide; it acts as a mentor for young creators aspiring to make an impact through their channels. By embracing authenticity, consistency, strategic planning, resilience against challenges, and continuous learning from both successes and setbacks, teenage boys can navigate their way towards becoming influential creators in the dynamic world of YouTube.

12.2 Staying Motivated Through Ups and Downs

The journey of a YouTube creator is fraught with highs and lows, successes and setbacks. Understanding how to maintain motivation through these fluctuations is crucial for long-term success and personal well-being. This exploration delves into strategies for staying motivated, drawing on insights from seasoned creators and psychological principles.

Motivation can wane when faced with criticism, stagnant growth, or creative blocks. However, several strategies can help creators navigate these challenges. Firstly, setting small, achievable goals can provide a sense of progress and accomplishment, fueling further efforts. Celebrating these milestones, no matter how minor they may seem in the grand scheme of things, reinforces positive behavior and builds resilience.

Another vital aspect is connecting with your community. Engagement from viewers—whether through comments, likes, or shares—can serve as a powerful motivator. Creators should foster this relationship by responding to feedback, involving viewers in content decisions through polls or Q&A sessions, and creating content that resonates with their audience's interests and needs.

- Reflecting on personal growth rather than just metrics can provide a more holistic view of success.
- Seeking inspiration from other creators without falling into the trap of comparison helps maintain a healthy perspective.
- Implementing a routine that includes breaks and time for hobbies outside of YouTube ensures balance and prevents burnout.

Beyond individual efforts, finding support from fellow YouTubers or joining creator communities can offer encouragement during tough times. Sharing experiences with those who understand the unique challenges of content creation provides not only practical advice but also emotional support.

In conclusion, staying motivated amidst the ups and downs requires a multifaceted approach that balances goal-setting with self-care, community engagement with personal reflection. By adopting these strategies, creators can sustain their passion for content creation over the long haul, turning obstacles into opportunities for growth and learning.

12.3 Looking Towards the Future

The journey of a YouTube creator is not just about navigating the present but also about looking forward and preparing for what lies ahead. As the digital landscape evolves, so too must creators adapt their strategies and content to stay relevant and continue growing their channels. This section explores key considerations for creators as they look towards the future, ensuring sustained success and relevance in an ever-changing online environment.

Understanding emerging trends is crucial for staying ahead in the competitive world of YouTube content creation. Creators must keep a keen eye on shifts in viewer preferences, platform updates, and broader societal changes that could impact how content is consumed. For instance, the rise of short-form video content has reshaped audience expectations, prompting many creators to diversify their content formats to include both long-form narratives and quick, engaging clips.

Technological advancements also play a significant role in shaping the future of YouTube content creation. Innovations such as augmented reality (AR), virtual reality (VR), and improved video editing software offer new avenues for creativity and storytelling. Embracing these technologies can help creators produce unique and immersive experiences for their viewers, setting them apart from competitors.

- Investing in learning new skills and technologies can enhance a channel's appeal and efficiency.
- Collaborating with other creators can open up new opportunities for growth and cross-promotion.
- Paying attention to changes in YouTube's algorithm and monetization policies ensures that creators can optimize their content strategy accordingly.

Beyond technology and trends, building a sustainable career on YouTube also means focusing on community building and personal branding. A strong connection with viewers fosters loyalty and increases engagement, while a clear personal brand helps differentiate a creator in a crowded market. As platforms evolve, these human elements remain constant drivers of success.

In conclusion, looking towards the future involves a combination of staying informed about industry trends, embracing technological advancements, continuously improving content quality, fostering community engagement, and refining personal branding strategies. By focusing on these areas, YouTube creators can navigate future challenges with confidence and continue to thrive in an ever-evolving digital landscape.

"How To Grow On YouTube As A Teenage Boy" serves as a comprehensive guide for young male creators aiming to carve out their niche on the YouTube platform. This non-fiction book is specifically designed to address the unique challenges and opportunities teenage boys encounter in the digital realm, offering a blend of practical advice, psychological insights, and industry secrets to aid in their journey towards becoming influential content creators. The book emphasizes the importance of authenticity, creativity, and consistency, presenting these elements as crucial for success on YouTube.

The guide covers a wide range of topics essential for budding YouTubers, including crafting relatable content that resonates with audiences, leveraging SEO strategies to enhance visibility, understanding analytics to gauge performance, and utilizing social media platforms for broader reach. It simplifies complex technical concepts for beginners while providing depth for more experienced creators seeking advanced tactics. Additionally, it tackles the psychological challenges young creators face, such as dealing with criticism and balancing commitments between school and YouTube.

Featuring interviews with successful YouTubers who began their careers as teenagers, the book offers real-life examples and motivational stories to inspire readers. These case studies illustrate that success on YouTube can be achieved through various paths. Practical exercises at the end of each chapter encourage readers to apply learned concepts directly to their channels, ensuring theoretical knowledge is translated into actionable steps.

In summary, "How To Grow On YouTube As A Teenage Boy" is an invaluable resource for any young boy embarking on a YouTube career. It not only provides tools for channel growth but also guides personal development in both digital and real-world contexts.

www.ingramcontent.com/pod-product-compliance
Lightning Source LLC
Chambersburg PA
CBHW070108230526
45472CB00004B/1162